Summer
Fruit

Summer Fruit

Sermons For Pentecost
(Middle Third)
Cycle C First Lesson Texts

Richard L. Sheffield

CSS Publishing Company, Inc.
Lima, Ohio

SUMMER FRUIT

Copyright © 1994 by
The CSS Publishing Company, Inc.
Lima, Ohio

Library of Congress Cataloging-in-Publication Data

Sheffield, Richard, 1947-
    Summer fruit : sermons for Pentecost (middle third) first lesson, cycle C / Richard Sheffield.
        p.   cm.
    ISBN 0-7880-0040-3
    1. Pentecost season—Sermons. 2. Bible. N.T. Gospels—Sermons. 3. Sermons, American. I. Title.
BV4300.5.S   1994
252'.6—dc20   94-1004
                                                                               CIP

This book is available in the following formats, listed by ISBN:
0-7880-0040-3 Book
0-7880-0041-1 IBM (3 1/2 and 5 1/4) computer disk
0-7880-0042-X IBM book and disk package
0-7880-0043-8 Macintosh computer disk
0-7880-0044-6 Macintosh book and disk package

PRINTED IN U.S.A.

For Xavia

*"One of Life's greatest successes
is to lose control of others
and gain control of yourself.*

*Life's greatest success
is to give control of yourself
to God."*

Xavia Arndt Sheffield

Table Of Contents

Foreword

Dick Sheffield is a stimulating preacher because he is at home in the real world of the 20th century and he can find his way on the back trails of holy scripture. No matter where he starts he can easily find his way back and forth between the Bible and modern culture.

These sermons echo the lyrics of the age and the vocabulary familiar to a contemporary high school student. Yet they also sound the high music of hope, love, forgiveness found in the passion of the Bible, as remembered by an older generation.

Dick is well read and not afraid to document his wide range of sources from classical theology to contemporary magazines. He is also a flesh and blood family man who experiences the spectrum of joy and frustration the rest of us endure.

If my own soul were dry I would read one of Dick's sermons and the springs of inspiration would start up again. His messages are not those you transpose as your own rearrangements. They are the encouragement, stimulation and provocation which ignite one's own soul's passion for the gospel and anger at injustices. After a while his devotional warmth and artful logic drive you to your own writing pad.

Dick Sheffield paints vivid pictures such as Jeremiah stuck in the mud in the bottom of the courtyard well or of himself caught in a traffic jam while he tries to rush home with a fresh pizza for the family. Whatever he describes, you find yourself there.

Part of the validity of Dick's freshness and sometimes radical acuteness is the integrity of the person who has had a sound religious experience and had it tested in modern banking at a level commensurate with his MBA degree. Everyone who reads the book will profit from his enthusiasm for Jesus Christ and life.

Rev. Bryant M. Kirkland, D.D.
Minister Emeritus
Fifth Avenue Presbyterian Church
New York City

Introduction

Good sermons are like good fruit, summer fruit. They are ripe — and ready to be consumed — for a short time. Then they go bad. Any preacher who has reached back in the "barrel" for a sermon when the week has been too busy to write a new one knows that. We find ourselves wondering, "Did I really say that?" If that has never happened, then we need to wonder whether we really said anything worth saying.

These sermons were prepared with two audiences in mind: my own congregation and other ministers who might find them useful. In so doing, I've not made the sermons "generic," preachable anytime, anyplace. Personal references and stories are still included. My assumption is that if someone chooses to preach one of these sermons "intact," they will be able to substitute their own experiences for mine. I would be flattered if someone actually made the effort to do that. I will have succeeded in my task if someone finds these words helpful in speaking God's Word to us all.

In reading the works of others, I've often wondered why they felt it was necessary to thank people the reader never heard of. But now I quickly realize my need to do the same.

Thanks to Mama and Daddy, Gladys and Louie Sheffield, and the congregation of the Buena Vista Road Assembly of God Church. Church for me was warmth and family before

11

it was theology and questions. When the questions came, we went different ways but hopefully we'll find ourselves at the same place "when the roll is called up yonder."

Much of the thanks I owe goes to congregations who have listened while I have learned. The Pompton Valley Presbyterian Church, Pompton Plains, New Jersey, where I had my first taste of ministry under the tutelage of Fred Anderson; and the Grace Presbyterian Church, Jenkintown, Pennsylvania, where Bill Murphey listened and helped me learn to listen to myself. They let this would-be preacher try his wings.

In particular I need to thank the congregations of the Presbyterian Church in Sudbury, Massachusetts, and the Market Street Presbyterian Church in Lima, Ohio, who have listened most of all during the 13 years since I was ordained.

Thanks also to the Fourth Presbyterian Church, Chicago, and the Fifth Avenue Presbyterian Church, New York City. Their warm and vital ministries, and the preaching and caring of Elam Davies and Bryant Kirkland made me a "Presbyterian" before I could even spell it. Bryant's ministry, and friendship, in particular, has nurtured my faith, my family, my calling, and my life. I blame Bryant for getting me into this, and thank him for helping make it possible.

Thanks to Jim McCord, the late President of Princeton Theological Seminary, who had a way of making everything seem possible; to Donald Macleod who taught me how to prepare to preach, and Arlo Duba who taught me the "catholic" tradition in which I try to do it. Thanks to that "great cloud of witnesses" in Seminary and congregations who have truly been "saints" in the Biblical sense of that word.

Most of all, though, thanks to the one person who has listened to more of my sermons than any other person on earth, my wife Xavia. She coached me, taught me, gently criticized me, but through it all, has loved and supported me. Whatever worth this little book has, we got here together.

Richard L. Sheffield
Lima, Ohio

October 12, 1993

Summer Fruit

Charles Swindoll says, "... it's a mad, bad, sad world."[1]
You *knew* that already?

He quotes Barbara Johnson who writes in her book *Splashes of Joy in the Cesspools of Life:* "The rain falls on the just and also on the unjust, but chiefly on the just, because the unjust steals the just's umbrella."[2]

The Prophet Amos, who lived and told it like it was about 750 years before the birth of Jesus, agreed with that assessment of life. There is a *lot* about this world that's mad or bad or sad or even "all of the above." And it falls on all of us, even the best of us, some of the time and sometimes all at the same time. But Amos' preaching was to Israel at a time when life for the nation of the people of God was actually "none of the above." It wasn't "mad, bad or sad" from their perspective. In fact, life made sense. Things were pretty good. And folks were happy to keep them that way, thank you very much!

Under King Jeroboam II life was as good as it ever was, and as good as it would ever be for these people who understood themselves to be the people of God. They were on top of the heap. It was into the midst of their peace and quiet that Amos came preaching gloom and doom. *The New Oxford Annotated Bible* says that "Amos was called by God from a

13

shepherd's task ... to the difficult mission of preaching harsh words in a smooth season." (To saying *out* loud what people knew *in*side but didn't want to hear about their lives.) "He denounced Israel, as well as its neighbors, for reliance upon military might, and for grave injustice in social dealings, abhorrent immorality, and shallow, meaningless piety."[3] As I read that I thought, there's a lot of that going around! Even 2,700 years later.

In the newspaper recently there was an article about ongoing debate in medical and world health circles, about what to do with the last vestiges of smallpox. This disease, which has killed millions, for thousands of years, has now been confined by medical science to some test tubes in a laboratory. It's completely under our control.

The debate is about whether we should now destroy all remaining remnants of the smallpox virus to insure that it will never, ever, for all time, destroy a human life again. Whether we dare even to continue to experiment with this deadly disease, when it's within our power to destroy it once and for all, is the now question. Think of it. We have come that far in knowing how to *protect* human life.

Yet, if you read Amos, and you read the rest of that same newspaper, it seems we have hardly moved at all in knowing how to *live* life. How to live life that's worth living forever. Amos could be preaching to us! To our time. To our nation. To our town. To our politics. To our business as usual. To our immorality. Even to our faith in God.

He is! And what Amos has to say is what Moses had to say hundreds of years before him; and what Jesus had to say hundreds of years after him; and what still needs to be said. We heard it read from the Gospel of Matthew. You can also find it in the Old Testament Book of Deuteronomy. "One does not live by bread alone" (by the things of this world alone, by politics and power and money and even piety alone), "but by every word that comes from the mouth of God" (Matthew 4:4; see also Deuteronomy 8:3).

14

What Moses warned the people not to do (which was to go any way but God's way), and what Jesus, we're told, was tempted to do (which was to have it his way instead of God's way), Amos said the people had done. In their politics, their business dealings, their morality, even their worship of God, they had gone their own way and done their own thing, and based their life on something other than "the words of the Lord" (Amos 8:11). That phrase may be taken to mean the *decalogue*, the ten words, the ten commandments, *The Words of the Lord*; the summary rules for life of the people of God.

Regarding those rules Moses had said to the people way back at Mount Sinai, right after the reading of the ten commandments: "You must . . . be careful to do as the Lord your God has commanded you; you shall not turn to the right or to the left. You must follow exactly the path that the Lord your God has commanded you, so that you may live, and that it may go well with you, and that you may live long in the land that you are to possess" (Deuteronomy 5:32-33).

Amos' word to the people is that they have turned from God's ways to other ways. And so they will die; ". . . the dead bodies shall be many, cast out in every place" (Amos 8:3). The end of this way of life, he says, is death! It's not a threat; it's a warning, that went unheeded. That a full life is more than a full stomach. Now I know, as well as you do, that it's easy to find people in this world for whom life is less than even a full stomach. But Amos is not talking to them. He's talking to people of means. Successful people, not unlike you and me. Among other things, Amos says the rich of Israel have taken advantage instead of taking care of those with less than a full stomach. They ". . . trample on the needy, and bring to ruin the poor of the land" (Amos 8:4).

In the paragraphs that I read Amos describes merchants, businessmen, on the sabbath, who couldn't wait for worship to be over so they could get back to business, and back to taking advantage of those less savvy about the ways of the marketplace than themselves. Those who wouldn't know they'd been shortchanged and overcharged. He doesn't just pick on

15

unethical businessmen who know how to short weights and pad accounts. But you'll have to read him for yourself to see who else he singles out.

But even as he singles out some of us, Amos is talking to all of us whose stomachs are full, whose bank accounts are full, whose calendars are full, *but whose lives are often empty*. They *look* full, says Amos, but they're like "... a basket of summer fruit" (Amos 8:1).

Amos' vision of what was happening to the nation of Israel, what Amos saw, what the Lord God showed him, was life that looks good, tastes good, and seems good. What Amos discerned is that a life that looks good but lacks goodness is on the verge of going bad.

In the vision Amos describes, God says: "... Amos, what do you see?" Amos says: "... a basket of summer fruit." God says: "The end has come upon my people ..." (Amos 8:1-2). It's a play on words in the Hebrew for "summer fruit" and "the end." Loosely translated it means: things are going from ripe to rotten in this basket.

That happens as easily with life as it does with my favorite summer (and winter!) fruit: a banana.

I like for a banana to be a rich golden color with tiny brown spots all over the peel. No green! The end should neither snap off, nor squish down, when you go to peel it. That's when it's ripe.

A banana at its best is good for about a day. And you can't control that. You can't put it in the refrigerator and preserve that. That just makes the peel brown, and the fruit mushy.

A good life is like a good banana. You can't preserve it for tomorrow; it's for today. And the question is not whether you get more of it, but what you do with what you have. One or two or even a dozen perfectly ripe bananas in a basket is a blessing. If all else fails, you make banana bread. But a whole truckload of perfectly ripe bananas would be a smelly disaster. More isn't always better, is the message of Amos.

What Amos is saying is that that which is good in life is like summer fruit — like a ripe banana — prone to rot if not eaten when it's time; prone to be a mess when taken to excess; prone to die if it's not lived as it should be.

Amos is not calling the people to account for being successful, which they were, but for being unfaithful and rotten to the core. For letting the good things of life become the gods of their lives. For breaking God's law as though the ten commandments were really the ten suggestions, to be kept at their convenience. The vision of summer fruit is a vision of life about to go bad — from ripe to rancid. Not because life was bad, but because they chose to live it badly.

The results of such living are laid out in uncomfortable detail throughout Amos' writings. The passage we read talks of death and mourning as the results of such a way of living. It even speaks of people going bald. I took that last as a touch of humor until I looked it up. Shaving the head was a way of mourning and grieving in Amos' day. No comic relief even there!

The passage also speaks of ". . . a famine . . . not a famine of bread, or a thirst for water, but of hearing the words of the Lord" (Amos 8:11). Not a hunger for food but a hunger for God that goes unsatisfied. A famine of the spirit.

Amos doesn't say that God quits speaking, but that we quit hearing after a while. That "amid all the changing words of our generation," we may not hear God's eternal word that does not change. The only word which speaks of life and of hope. A word spoken most clearly to us in the life, death, and resurrection of Jesus Christ.

The people of Israel didn't like what they heard. They liked how they lived. They wouldn't listen. They ran Amos out of town. He went home and wrote it all down. In hopes that someday, somewhere, someone would hear the Word of the Lord about the way to live with him and with each other — and then live it — now and forever.

---

1. Charles Swindoll. *Laugh Again* (Word Publishers, 1992) p. 171.

2. *Ibid.*

3. *The New Oxford Annotated Bible* (Oxford University Press, 1991) p. 1170 O.T.

Gomer,
God's "Yet"

For everybody who assumed that everybody in the Bible is nice, the message this morning is that *everybody in the Bible is **real**, and God loved them anyway!*

Our subject this morning is Gomer. Not Gomer, Ohio, but the not-so-nice wife of the Prophet Hosea. I have never preached about Gomer before. And, quite honestly, I probably would not be preaching about her now, except that I have to.

The CSS Publishing Company, here in Lima, has asked me to publish a book of sermons next spring on the Old Testament lessons for the middle of next summer. The story I read is one of them. The only way to get this done is to preach the lessons in the middle of this summer. So here we are hoping to hear God's word in this story about Hosea and Gomer.

Because we live in northwest Ohio, the first thing I need to tell you is that Gomer, Ohio, less than half-an-hour from here, was not named for Hosea's wife, Gomer. Gomer, Ohio, was named for Noah's grandson, Gomer, who is the traditional ancestor of the Welsh people (Genesis 10:2). Actually it would've been a better story if it *had* been named for Hosea's wife and I was hoping, but our church member, Martha Evans, a lifelong resident of Gomer set me straight.

19

Hosea's wife, Gomer, was not nice. I'm trying to be nice. She was a woman of "ill-repute," of bad reputation. And she continued as such even after she got married to Hosea. In the part of the story we read from the Book of Hosea, we hear of the birth of three children to Gomer: a son, Jezreel; a daughter, Lo-ruhamah; a son, Lo-ammi. They were Gomer's children; they were not Hosea's. The children's names had meanings. The kids, in effect, became Hosea's outline for a three-point sermon on the condition of the people of Israel.

Jezreel, the name of the first son, means, literally, "God sows," as in sowing seeds in a field. And just as in the cornfields and beanfields out near Gomer, Ohio, what has been sown is what will be reaped. The message is that the sins of the people (who are represented by Gomer in the story) will be the harvest of the people. "What you sow is what you get" is the message of the name of this first child.

The daughter's name is Lo-ruhamah, which means "not pitied." The *New Oxford Annotated Bible* says: "Because of Israel's sin the Lord will *no longer have pity,* and the name of the second child will be a living reminder of this."[1] God has lost patience with people who are compared in the way they lived to the way Gomer made her living.

There will be no pity from God for what they are about to get for the sins they have done. They're getting what they deserve. They have done what they ought not to have done, and they have not done what they ought to have done. And as Paul taught in the New Testament ". . . the wages of sin is death . . ." (Romans 6:23). In naming the second child Lo-ruhamah God's saying: "Tough! You reap what you sow, don't expect me to be sorry."

The third child is Lo-ammi. A son whose name is most fearful of all. The relationship of Israel to God is a covenant relationship. It's based on a promise. God will be their God and the people will be God's people. That's the deal.

In Exodus it says that God said to the people gathered on Mount Sinai: "Now therefore, if you obey my voice and keep my covenant, you shall be my treasured possession out of all the peoples. Indeed, the whole earth is mine, but you shall be for me a priestly kingdom and a holy nation'' (Exodus 19:5-6). God's part of the deal, the covenant, is to be their God. The people's part is to be his people. And all the promises and blessings promised as far back as the beginning of Israelite history with the call of Abraham, God will deliver. Except now, the word from God, in the name of this third child, Lo-ammi, is ''. . . you are not my people and I am not your God'' (Hosea 1:9). *Deal's off!*

Because of the way they are living, personified by the way Gomer was living, the people of God, the children of God, to whom God had promised everything, have apparently been disowned. They'll get nothing. ''Name him Lo-ammi (God said), for you are not my people and I am not your God'' (Hosea 1:9).

Hosea's relationship with his wayward wife is really a story about God's relationship with his wayward people. And the intimacy of God's relationship with us, expressed in the New Testament in Jesus' calling God ''Father,'' and teaching us to do the same, is expressed in Hosea in the intimacy of Hosea's troubled marriage. God's relationship with his people is like Hosea's relationship with his wife. And both are marriages one expects to be over.

God has said: ''You get what you deserve in this life. I don't have any reason to feel the least bit sorry for you. And I'm out of here!''

Those are Hosea's three points, Gomer's three children. It's over!

Yet!

Yet!

That's the most helpful word in the whole Bible: *yet!* Which simply means ''it ain't over 'til it's over, and it ain't over *yet!*'' In spite of all that's been said, and all that's been done, God says: *''Yet* the number of the people of Israel shall be like the sand of the sea, which can be neither measured nor numbered; and in the place where it was said to them, 'you are not my people,' it shall be said to them, 'children of the living God' '' (Hosea 1:10).

The conclusion to this "living sermon" is a reaffirmation of God's promise that he *will* be their God and they *will* be his people. God had said to Abraham, "I will indeed bless you, and I will make your offspring as numerous as the stars of heaven and as the sand that is on the seashore" (Genesis 22:17). The message in Hosea is you may become a people as wayward as Hosea's wife, *yet* I will still love you. I have every reason not to, but I *will* be your God, and you *will* be my people, in spite of you, because I love you!

In the midst of Hosea's reporting the bad news about us, there is a newsflash reporting the good news about God.

The conclusion to his three-point, three-kid sermon is not the one you expect. It *isn't* over, *yet!* Because God's love never ends. Because God's love is like the love in the hymn we sing: ". . . love that wilt not let (you and) me go."[2]

So in the midst of our lives lived like the unfaithful Gomer, we can still sing "Great is thy faithfulness, O God my Father . . . Great is thy faithfulness, Lord, unto me."[3] As unfaithful as we may be — God is faithful always in his love. Like Hosea with his wife, he keeps bringing us back.

"A Brief Statement of Faith" adopted by The Presbyterian Church several years ago puts our relationship with God this way:

> We trust in God,
>   whom Jesus called Abba, Father.
> In sovereign love God created the world good
>   and makes everyone equally in God's image,
>   male and female, of every race and people,
>   to live as one community.
> But we rebel against God; we hide from our creator.
>   Ignoring God's commandments,
>   we violate the image of God in others and ourselves,
>   accept lies as truth,
>   exploit neighbor and nature,
>   and threaten death to the planet entrusted to our care.
> We deserve God's condemnation.

YET

> *God acts with justice and mercy to redeem creation.*
>> *In everlasting love,*
>>> *the God of Abraham and Sarah chose a covenant*
>>>> *people to bless all families of the earth.*
>> *Hearing their cry,*
>>> *God delivered the children of Israel*
>>>> *from the house of bondage.*
>> *Loving us still,*
>>> *God makes us heirs with Christ of the covenant.*
>> *Like a mother who will not forsake her nursing child,*
>> *like a father who runs to welcome the prodigal home,*
>> *God is faithful still.*[4]

We deserve God's condemnation, *YET* God is faithful still. That's the message of Hosea.

The book of Hosea makes interesting reading. Its teaching is simple. In spite of our unfaithfulness to all that is good and true, in spite of our unfaithfulness to ourselves, and to one another, and even to God, *God is always faithful to you and me.*

The way we live has real and sometimes unhappy consequences for the life we have. We know that.

YET,

> *with believers in every time and place,*
> *we can rejoice that nothing in life or in death*
> *can separate us from the love of God*
>> *in Christ Jesus our Lord.*[5]

---

1. *The New Oxford Annotated Bible* (Oxford University Pressy, 1991) p. 1149 OT.

2. *Presbyterian Hymnal* 384 (Westminster/John Knox Press, 1990).

3. *Presbyterian Hymnal* 276.

4. "A Brief Statement of Faith," *The Book of Confessions,* Presbyterian Church (U.S.A.)

5. *Ibid.*

Where Are You?

Where are you?

Do you know?

It's actually possible to be sitting here, but still *be* somewhere else! It's also possible to live that way. Do you know where you are; are you where you *need* to be in your life?

Occasionally at mealtimes at our house, especially when it's been a long and busy day and I'm distracted, Xavia will say *"Dick!* Where are you?" I'm sitting there. I'm eating there. But I'm not there. I'm still at my meeting, I'm still at the hospital, I'm anywhere but where I *need* to be at that moment. Your mind can wander off while your body stays put.

Communication specialists tell us that the most important thing and the hardest thing about good communication is being where the person you're talking with is. If you aren't there with them communication doesn't happen. If, instead of listening to what they are saying, you're busy planning what you're going to say in response, you aren't really there.

So where are you as you listen to this sermon, as you worship God, *as you live your life?*

One way to get at where you are is to look at where you *were:* where you've been. We got where we *are* from somewhere else. Where was that? Someone has said, "Success isn't how far you got, but the distance you traveled from where

25

you started'' (Source unknown). Where'd you start? Where were you 70 years ago, seven years ago, or even seven *days* ago? Where were you last Monday? Do you know? Maybe not. That's not so long ago, but unless something "memorable" happened, you may not remember the ordinary things that were part of getting you to where you are now. But think about it for a minute. Where were you last Monday?

I know exactly where I was hour by hour! And I know now that I was exactly where I needed to be. At 3 a.m. last Monday I was getting out of bed. At 3:45 a.m. I was driving to Columbus. At 6:40 a.m. I was on a jet to New York City. At 8:15 a.m. I was landing at LaGuardia Airport. At 9:15 a.m. I was getting off the bus at 42nd Street in midtown Manhattan.

At 9:30 a.m. I was buying a baker's dozen bagels at the Essa Bagel Shop on Third Avenue. At 9:45 I was trying to find the men's room at Rockefeller Center. At 10:00 a.m. I was in a pew in the Lady Chapel at St. Patrick's Cathedral. At the other end of the pew, by coincidence, was an old friend I hadn't seen in 15 years. Richard had lost most of the hair on the top of his head. I had lost all the hair on my top lip. So it took us a while to recognize each other. I was there because one of the best friends I ever had, the best man at our wedding, had died. I was there, we were there, to say good-bye.

At about 11:00, having shared in the sacrament we will share in a few minutes, that makes us one in Christ with all who have gone before us, and with each other; having given thanks for Matthew's life, and his part in my life; I went across 50th Street to that other place that symbolizes where we are in our lives (and maybe in our worship for that matter) — Saks Fifth Avenue. Jenny wanted something from Saks. I brought her a shopping bag. If you saw the price tags you'd know why I quickly decided that *wasn't* where I should be.

By 11:30 I was at Matthew's apartment for the last time. Visiting, remembering, meeting others in his life I had never known. Over the years we'd grown apart. Our lives were in 1993, but our friendship was in 1983. Where we were wasn't where we had been. So I caught up with Matt through others of his friends.

26

At 1:00 I was in a cab heading back to LaGuardia. At 2:10 I was on the way — to Baltimore. At 4:00 I was sitting in a hot plane on the ground in Baltimore listening to the pilot explain that they couldn't get the engines started! At 4:45, having been reassured that the problem was the ground generator, not the plane, we took off. At 5:35 I was in Columbus. At 7:40 I kissed my kids goodnight. At 8:00 the session met here at the church. At 10:30 I kissed Xavia goodnight, and went to sleep.

That's where *I* was. And it was where *I* needed to be last Monday. That's what I told Matt's brother; I came because that was where I needed to be. Where were *you* and where are you now? Where have you been in your life? Have you stayed put, or moved on? Have you moved ahead to what can be, or tried to go back to what could've been? Are you where you need to be?

This is not a message full of easy answers; it's a message full of hard questions, because that's what life is like. How we answer the questions determines how we live our lives. That was true for my friend Matt. It's true for me. It's true for you. Our lives are our answers to life's questions.

But the basic question of the Bible is not that of those who try to scare people into heaven by scaring the hell out of them. Asking questions like "If you were to die tonight where would you be tomorrow?" The basic question of the Bible and of life is, "If you *don't* die tonight, where will you be tomorrow, and the day after, and the day after that?" And is that where you want and need to be?

The biblical story, like the passage I read from Hosea, is remembered not because God told it, but because people who knew God lived it. Like I lived Monday and remembered it because it had an effect on my life, on where I am now. The Bible helps us see where we are through the eyes of the faithful (and the not-so-faithful) who've been there before.

Someone once said: "Learn from the mistakes of others; you can't live long enough to make them all yourself" (Source unknown). Some of us try anyway! But the Bible calls us to

27

learn from the mistakes of all those people you thought were perfect like Moses, and David, and Isaiah, and Jeremiah, and even the 12 disciples. To learn from their lives, and our lives, as we live them where *we* are right now.

I haven't forgotten Hosea. Hosea was a prophet who lived about 700 years before Jesus was born. Biblical prophets aren't seers or fortune-tellers, writing in riddles so you and I can figure out tomorrow. They don't "tell it like it will be," so much as they "tell it like it is." Hosea, and others like him, confronted the people of God with where they *were* with God. And also with where God was with them. The people were not where they were supposed to be, where they needed to be in their relationship with God. And they were going the wrong way to get there. "The more I called them (to go the *right* way, says God) the more they went from me . . . My people are bent on turning away from me (on going their own way)" (Hosea 11:2, 7).

If "success (in life) isn't how far you got, but the distance you traveled from where you started," *failure* in life isn't how far you got, either, but whether you went the right way. Whether where you are is closer to where you need to be than when you started is the measure of our hours and our days.

Hosea's message to the people was you're not where you should be and you're going the wrong way to get there. Throughout Hosea, and all the prophets, are lots of harsh words about where that will get you. And you can pretty much sum up their words in one word: hell, here or hereafter. I really wonder which is worse: the burning hell of theology or the living hell of too many lives. Whichever, that isn't where we want or have to be.

But life can go to hell when we go the wrong way in our living. And which way is that? Any way but God's way. Jesus summed up God's way in one word: love. Love God, Love your neighbor, and live, said Jesus. It is in our loving that we live a life worth living now and forever. It's in our loving that we live like God and find Christ in our lives.

Hosea describes the way to live, by describing the way God loves. It's "in-spite-of" love. Love that goes on loving even the most unlovable. Love that loves you no matter where you are. Hosea says that this is the nature of God: that the heat of God's anger becomes the warmth of God's love.

The good news of the gospel is not that you get what you've got coming, but that God is coming to get you and hold you in his arms. In spite of all the wrong that God's people had done, says Hosea, God still said: "How can I give you up . . .? My heart recoils within me (at the thought); my compassion grows warm and tender. I will not execute my fierce anger; . . . For I am God and no mortal, the holy one in your midst, and I will not come in wrath" (Hosea 11:8-9, adapted).

God does not come to where we are in anger, but in love and forgiveness. That's where God is coming from. That's where God is. Where are you? Where *are* you, in your loving, and in the living of your life? Wherever it is, one thing is sure, God loves you and he's right there with you.

Let's Live

Okay, people; let's get with it!

> *"Hear the word of the Lord ...*
> *Listen to the teaching of our God ...*
> *(because) I have had enough ... I am weary ...*
> *and I will not listen ..." (Isaiah 1:10-15)*
> *(anymore)! "Let us argue it out ... now ..."*
>   *(Isaiah 1:18)*

Then let's get with it!

Thus says the Lord our God, speaking through the mouth of his prophet Isaiah, to his people: people who didn't get it then and people who "still don't get it now." Actually I think we *do* get it; we just don't get around to getting it done, do we? Living as God says to live?

God says: "... Cease to do evil, learn to do good; seek justice, rescue the oppressed, defend the orphan, plead for the widow" (Isaiah 1:16-17). (If you don't) "What to me is the multitude of your sacrifices?" (Isaiah 1:11). Don't just pray about it, do something about it. Do what you pray and do not pray for what you will not do! *C'mon; let's get with it, shall we?*

31

Isaiah, God's prophet, (and by the way, a prophet is not someone who tells you how it's going to be so much as someone who tells it like it is): Isaiah doesn't mince words; and neither does God. Confronted with words like Isaiah's words to the people of Israel, it is all too easy for us to reply: "Boy, God really had it in for them, didn't he? I wonder what they did, or didn't do?"

But as Henry Sloane Coffin, writing in *The Interpreter's Bible,* notes: "...the word of God has a most perturbing way of disregarding dates and of making truth contemporary."[1]

It's always important in reading the scriptures to be sure you know *what it said* to those who heard it said for the first time. We need to understand the historical context, the situation of the people involved, the meaning of the metaphors and allusions for them, the reality of life then to which the scriptures spoke then.

But that done, we need to understand in our own history, in our own situation, the meaning of the metaphors and allusions, and the reality of life *now*, to which the scriptures speak *now.*

What kind of world is it in which *we* live? What is it *we* are supposed to do in that world? What is God's word to *us?*

One author notes: "In the tradition of Amos, Hosea, and Micah (other prophets of Israel), contemporaries whose work Isaiah seems to know, Isaiah attacks social injustice as that which is most indicative of Judah's tenuous relationship with God. He exhorts his hearers to place their confidence in their omnipotent God and to lead such public and private lives as manifest this."[2]

In other words, God says through Isaiah: *"Don't pray if you won't do!!"* For "... even though you make many prayers, I will not listen" (Isaiah 1:15). In our prayers our God does want to hear what we need, and what we have to say, but he also wants to hear what we want *to do.* And not just about our needs, but about the needs of all God's children.

That's a mouthful; God intends it to be an earful! He says: *"Listen* ... for the mouth of the Lord has spoken" (Isaiah

1:10, 20). And then he listens for what we speak with what we do. He listens to how we pray. He hears us pray: "... Your kingdom come your will be done on earth as in heaven ...." And then he watches and listens to see what on earth we're going to do to make that happen.

Someone once quipped that Christians are often "too heavenly minded to be any earthly good." Isaiah is trying to bring us down to earth where we can do some good, for God's sake — and for our sake, and for the sake of others.

Now don't get me wrong. That doesn't mean we haven't done any good. On the contrary, the church, Market Street Presbyterian Church, has done a lot of good. Isaiah's "thus says the Lord" doesn't say we haven't done good. But rather that "God is always calling us to *be* more than we have been."[3] To *do* more than we have done.

As Frederick Buechner puts it, God is calling you "... to begin to hear something not only of who you are but of both what you are becoming and what you are failing to become."[4]

We're called, you and I, as Isaiah was called: to speak a word of truth about our world, our town, and ourselves. We may not be called to speak it so vigorously, or so loudly, or so angrily as Isaiah.

But if we leave here week after week believing that we were simply called here to *hear* the truth then we leave here without the truth. For truth is not just in saying the right words, or in understanding the right theories, or even in believing the right doctrines of the church. *Truth is in doing the right thing* whether what we're doing is worshipping within these walls, or living beyond them.

I heard a speaker recently say that many of us live by "don't plans," instead of "do plans." Too many of us live our faith that way, too. We look at the ten commandments as God's "don't plan." Trouble is "don't plans" don't work! And that's easy to prove.

For example, right now, no matter what you do, *don't* think of a red convertible! What are you thinking about? We say to our kids, "Don't run!" Why not say to them, "walk!"

33

The message of the Bible is not a simple "don't do this, that, and the other thing." It's *do this and live!*

What's your "do plan?" What do you want to do?

For Isaiah the people of Israel were doing all the right things at church and all the wrong things everywhere else which made even the right things the wrong things to do. All those sacrifices and rituals were the right things to do but they became the wrong things to do because of what else they did and did not do. Their worship was not pleasing to God because the way they lived was not pleasing to God.

In their day, as in ours, there was a dangerous separation between prayer and practice, between worship and worldly activities, between what people "believed" and what people did.

We could excuse that way of living by arguing that after all we're only human. And that's the way we humans live. The Apostle Paul said once: ". . . I do not do the good I want, but the evil I do not want is what I do" (Romans 7:19).

And even Jesus was tempted to do things his way instead of doing them God's way in his sojourn with the devil in the desert. The devil said: "A little power, a little prestige, a little money, Jesus; you can have it all, if you do things my way." And Jesus could have said, "The devil made me do it." Then he could have gone to church and confessed along with everyone else: ". . . We have left undone those things which we ought to have done; and we have done those things we ought not to have done . . ."[5]

God knows, that's true, at least for me. But it isn't the truth God has for me — or you. And it's certainly no way to live! Because "what we ought to have done" is what we *need* to have done to meet *our* needs, as well as the needs of others. And "what we ought not to have done" — but did — is anything we did which caused us or someone else unnecessary pain.

I recently had the opportunity to judge a speech contest for high school students at the Rotary Club. The assigned topic for these young people was how do you *do* what Rotarians say they believe?

Rotarians say they believe that life should be lived by "the four-way test of the things we think, say or do." It asks four questions about anything you do:

1. *Is it the truth?* Simple question. Is it true? If it isn't, stop there.

2. *Is it fair to all concerned?* Even if it is true, is it *fair?* Is there some balance in this? If not don't do it!

3. *Will it build goodwill and better friendships?* Even if it is true and everybody's treated "equally," will it build goodwill? Will it make us friends? Will we still be friends? No? Then it isn't worth it!

4. *Will it be beneficial to all concerned?* Even if it is true, and we're all agreed it's fair, and we'll still be friends, will it benefit *everybody* concerned? Does anybody get the short end of the stick on this? If so, you need to take another look at what you're doing.

Christians believe a lot *more* than that. But the question is: *How often do we do less than that?*

Those young people talked about how living that — *doing* that — just *that* — would make for better schools, better communities, a better world, and better lives for us all. Judging the contest was hard. That means there's hope, that if their generation can manage to *do* what they *say* our world can be a better place for us all.

Isaiah wasn't trying to win a speech contest. He was trying to win people over to living the life that God intends for us all. To the kind of life and the kind of world described in Isaiah's words now carved into a wall across from the United Nations in New York City. A city which has just known the kind of mindless death and destruction that comes from not living God's way, or even Rotary's way.

Isaiah described a world in which: "They shall beat their swords into plowshares, and their spears into pruning hooks; nation shall not lift up sword against nation, neither shall they learn war any more" (Isaiah 2:4).

That's the kind of world, the kind of community, the kind of life, that we want for our young people; that we want for our kids; that we need for ourselves. We can only have it if we want it for everybody.

Do we get it?
Then let's get with it!
Let's *do* it!
Let's live!

---

1. *The Interpreter's Bible* (Abingdon Press, 1956) "Isaiah," p. 172.

2. *The New Oxford Annotated Bible* NRSV (Oxford University Press, 1991) p. 866 O.T.

3. Loren B. Mead. *The Once And Future Church* (Alban Institute, 1991).

4. Frederick Buechner. *Listening To Your Life* (San Francisco: Harper, 1992) p. 56.

5. *The Book of Common Worship* (Westminster/John Knox Press, 1993) p. 21.

Some
Good News

Finally! There's some *good* news!

In a March 23, 1993 *Lima News* report, in the midst of the latest news from Texas, and the latest reports from New York, and the latest atrocity stories from the former Yugoslavia, comes this: "Forget oat bran or garlic. The new wonder food may be walnuts."

I'm one of those people who gave up regular coffee for decaffeinated coffee; and then gave up coffee for tea; and then gave up tea for herbal tea; and then went back to regular coffee; all on the basis of bad news about what was good for me. I'm often frustrated by the fact that so many of the things that *taste* good, aren't good *for* me; so this latest bit of good news, tucked in on page B-10 of the newspaper, after all the bad news, was welcome news to me.

I like walnuts; and apparently, walnuts like me! Says the article in the *News:* "Unlikely as it may sound, a study released today suggests that nuts in general, and walnuts in particular, lower cholesterol." That's good news. Now, if they can just figure out that it's okay to eat my walnuts with vanilla ice cream, chocolate sauce, whipped cream, and maraschino cherries on the side.

But did you hear the way the Associated Press reporter led into his story? I read it. Did you hear it? It says something

about our world and our town and our lives. He wrote: *"Unlikely as it may sound* ... there's some *good* news (we think)."
He hedges, but we *think* the news is good, "unlikely as it may sound." Why is that so unthinkable, so unlikely? Why am I waiting for the report that says that walnuts *will* lower my cholesterol but also will make my hair fall out faster and give me some other condition I can't even pronounce? Is that just me? Or are you just as guilty of looking at life that way, at least part of the time?

I've often heard it said of the weather in Ohio: "If you don't like it wait an hour, it will change." That carries over into how we see life: "If you don't like it wait, it will get worse."

I'm reading a new book called *Divorce Busting*. Michelle Weiner-Davis writes in the context of our personal lives something that is true of all of our lives. She writes that the negative "... perspective (seems to) shield you from the pain and disappointment of trying unsuccessfully to find happiness again. You tell yourself, 'If I expect the worst, I won't be disappointed.' Right? No (she says), wrong! Norman Cousins said, 'We fear the worst, we expect the worse, we invite the worst.' Simply, if you expect the worst, you'll get it."[1]

She talks about an experiment with school-age children. Educators came in and gave all the children an IQ test. Then they selected children *at random* and told the teachers that these were children from whom they could expect the best work. They were not necessarily the children with the highest IQs. But at the end of the grading period they were the children who achieved the most — based simply on the expectations that the teachers had of them.

We need to look at our expectations of ourselves and others. Quit giving the front page of life to the bad news, and burying the good news on Section B, page 10, where it's all too easy to overlook. The bad stuff will get your attention no matter where it is, so put the good stuff up front.

Dr. Bryant Kirkland, now serving as the interim pastor at The National Presbyterian Church in Washington, D.C., told me that when I was still in seminary. He said, "Dick, when you're getting ready to preach remember that *they know the bad news*; they came to hear some good news. It's your job to tell them!" Put the good stuff up front!

Just think. If every preacher, including this one, always preached like that; if every Christian always lived like that, in church and out, what a world, what a town, what a church, what a life, this would be! It might even be worth living — forever.

The Old Testament prophet Isaiah, the son of Amoz, had a lot to say about life and the way we live it. We've come to use the word "prophet" to mean someone who tells us how life *will* be. The Bible uses the word "prophet" to mean *someone who tells it like it is* ... which is the same as telling it like it will be if nothing changes. Isaiah, and all the prophets of God, have one simple message: "If you *keep* going the way you've *been* going you'll eventually get there" (Source unknown).

Question is: *Is that where you want to get?* And the prophets' call to repentance, a call to acknowledging who we are and what we're like — the bad stuff we need to confront and confess — is not a call to getting forgiven while you keep on going the same old way. It's a call to changing direction (the literal meaning of "repent") and going a different way in your life. Jesus said to his followers at one point in his teaching: "I am the way ...." Go my way for a change in your life.

One way to change your direction, is to change your expectations. And put the good stuff up front *for a change!*

When I was learning to drive, my father said I should never look directly into the headlights of oncoming cars because what you look at is what you go toward, and on a highway at night that would be dangerous. It's just as dangerous to always look at what's wrong, what's bad, what's not what it could be, on the highway we call life. No one can do that and live. We need to put some good stuff up front for a change in our lives.

Isaiah does that in the passage I read but you may have missed it. I'll bet you heard the bad stuff loud and clear. *The New Oxford Annotated Bible* calls the poetry of Isaiah 5:1-7 "song of the vineyard." What kind of song is it? A song of despair? Isaiah sounds like Nancy Sinatra in a song popular in the '60s: "One of these days these boots are gonna' walk all over you . . ." Just expect it! One of these days God's gonna' tromp all over you!

The vineyard (which is a metaphor for life) has been carefully planted and tended by the owner who is God. He planted it in good soil; he removed the stones, kept watch so that no one would vandalize it or steal the grapes, and built a vat in expectation of tromping grapes and making good wine. He had high hopes for it. But it went to pot. The grapes grew wild and bitter. And the owner says, basically, "To heck with it." Let's be theologically correct. He said: "To hell with it!" Because such a vineyard, such a life, *is* hell: devoured by despair, trampled down by trivial pursuits, overgrown with sour grapes, and dry as dust on the road to nowhere.

Isaiah wants to make sure we understand the meaning of the song so he writes: "Israel is the vineyard of the Lord Almighty; the people of Judah are the vines he planted. He expected them to do what was good, but instead they committed murder. He expected them to do what was right, but their victims cried out for justice" (Isaiah 5:7, GNB). That's the translation of the *Good News Bible*. Sounds like the *good* news is the *bad* news about us, because *we* are the people of God. We are the ones God calls to do good and do right. The vineyard is life, and we are planted here to live it. Isaiah says God wants what is good, God wants what is right, God gets "sour grapes," *and so do we!*

It's easy to get defensive about this. "I haven't murdered anyone; I haven't oppressed or victimized anyone!" Maybe not, but have you been angry with anyone? Jesus said, "You've heard it said don't murder? I say don't be angry." Have you used anyone to get what you wanted? Have you been used? Then you understand what it means to be oppressed. Isaiah knew the bad stuff of life, as well as you and I do, and he wrote about it for pages; but in the midst of being honest about life, he put the good stuff up front.

Right at the beginning of the song he says, "Let me sing for my beloved my love-song concerning his vineyard . . ." *It's a love song!* It's an honest song but it's sung in love. Even in his anger, even in his frustration, even in his readiness to wreak havoc in this relationship with his people, *God is in love!* That's why Isaiah's word wasn't the last word God had to say. Because the first word, the word God puts up front, is *love.* Before he says, "I'd like to tell you about yourself," God says, "I'd like to tell you I love you. I'm going to tell you about yourself *because* I love you."

I believe it was the evangelist Leighton Ford who is quoted as saying: "God loves you just the way you are, but he loves you too much to leave you that way." So in the words of Isaiah and the words of Jesus he shows you and me a new way. A new way to live.

One note of caution. That does *not* mean that the way to relate to your spouse, or to your child, or to your co-worker, or to your friend, is to say, "I love you, now let me tell you about you." What God has to say judges us all. But what I have to say judges me. In our relationships with one another, be it nation with nation, city with township, husband with wife, parent with child, or just you and me, what we need is love. What we need to do, up front, is love, as Jesus loved.

> Love the Lord our God,
> each other
> and ourselves.
> Because *"unlikely as it may sound . . ."*
> up front, before anything else,
> before any of the bad news about you and me,

the *good* news is:
God loves you and me.

---

1. Michelle Weiner-Davis. *Divorce Busting* (Simon and Schuster, 1992) p. 45.

What's The Point?

In the church we used to teach the Christian Faith in the form of a catechism. That's a question and answer format which when learned gives basic answers to basic questions about Christian belief and living a Christian life. The catechism was meant to be memorized like the multiplication table, so that at least some of life's questions might have answers as quickly as we know $2 \times 2 = 4$. Interestingly, the latest General Assembly has proposed writing a new Catechism to help us to ask the right questions and find the right answers to living life as God intends it to be lived.

The larger Catechism, found in the *Book of Confessions* of the Presbyterian Church (U.S.A.), has as its *first* question, the first thing to learn about how to live, *this* question: "What is the chief and highest end of man?" Modern Version: What's the point of my life. Answer: "Man's chief and highest end is to glorify God, and fully to enjoy him forever."[1] Before all else in life, what life is all about, now and forever, for you and for me is glorifying and enjoying the God who made us.

We used to assume that every Presbyterian learned that along the way. Perhaps we need to learn it again.

The 19th century hymnwriter Fanny Crosby put it this way: "To God be the Glory, great things He hath done! ... Praise the Lord, Praise the Lord, Let the People Rejoice!"[2] Give

43

Glory to God and be joyful; that's what life is all about. And as Saint Irenaeus put it in the 2nd century: "The Glory of God is a human being who is fully alive."[3] Simply put, *the purpose of life is living — joyfully!*

So why don't we just *say* that?

Perhaps because we find it so hard to *do* that.

For whatever reason, the Bible calls whatever reason it is *sin*. Human beings have a heck of a time being happy beings. And that's a sin! That may be *the* sin!

Someone once observed that when our living this life is done, the one thing God will hold us most accountable for is our having failed to enjoy all the good things he made for us. Having failed to live life glorifying him by the way we live, and enjoying it.

Jeremiah, a preacher's kid who grew up to be a prophet, tells us in the passage I read from his writings how we might learn to do better; and not just for God — for ourselves. In those opening lines from his book Jeremiah had condensed into a brief dialogue between himself and God the spiritual struggles and spiritual insights of a lifetime. It didn't happen one morning over breakfast, but over many years. And so, I suspect, it will be for us.

In summary the passage comes to this: what God said. What Jeremiah said. What God said. All the rest of Jeremiah's book is about what happened.

It starts with God. It always does. As an unknown poet put it: "I sought the Lord, and afterward I knew he moved my soul to seek him, seeking me; it was not I that found, O Saviour true, no I was found of Thee."[4]

When God had found Jeremiah what he had to say is recorded in some of the most beautiful language in all scripture: "Now the word of the Lord came to me (said Jeremiah) saying, 'Before I formed you in the womb I knew you, and before you were born I consecrated you; I appointed you a prophet to the nations' " (Jeremiah 1:4-5). Think about that, Jeremiah! Jeremiah did. His response is my second point.

But first, you and I need to think about that. Think about it! The God of all creation knew *you* and *me* before we were created. He had intimate knowledge (that's what it means "to know") and intimate understanding of you and me before there was a you and me. And he has big plans, big ideas, big hopes and big dreams, for you and me. There is meaning and purpose in life. And God has something in mind for each of us.

I know it doesn't always seem like it. And sometimes it may seem that what God has in mind, you'd rather forget. But let me suggest that sin and the pain it brings, in our lives, be it personal or international, is what happens to us when God's purpose is not what's happening in our lives; when life is *not* as God intends it to be.

I've often sat in my study listening to someone in physical pain or in a painful situation ask, "Why is God doing this to me?" The simplest answer: *He isn't!* "Is this what God has in mind for me?" Answer: *No!* The God who knew you before he made you, whose concern and relationship with you is such that Jesus would later teach that "... even the hairs of your head are all counted" by him (Matthew 10:30). This God is not out to do you in. He's out to do big things in your life. He knew you before you were born.

He knows you now. He knows your need. He knows the possibilities in your life. And he wants you to see them, too.

He knew Jeremiah: "I appointed you a prophet to the nations" (Jeremiah 1:5). God didn't ask Jeremiah to consider the position and get back to him; he said, you had the job before you were born.

That may make you and me a bit uncomfortable. Shouldn't God *ask* me? He does. And very often we turn him down. But he keeps the job open while you and I look around and look for the meaning of our lives.

Sometime after we're born we begin to ask, "What is the meaning in my life." As Rabbi Kushner puts it, there comes a point in life where we ask: "Was there something I was supposed to do with my life?"[5] Kushner writes: "The need for meaning is not a biological need like the need for food and air. Neither is it a psychological need, like the need for acceptance and self esteem. It is a religious need, *an ultimate thirst of our souls.*[6] You and I need to know more than how to make a living. We need to know the *meaning* of our living, if we're to truly live. We need to know what God has in mind for our lives. Not how God is manipulating me to get what he wants; but what does God have in mind for me that will give me what I want, which is to live a life full of joy.

The search for meaning is a search for the mind of God.

God spoke his mind to Jeremiah: I know you better than you know yourself, and "I appointed you a prophet to the nations."

Jeremiah said, "Ah, Lord God! Truly I do not know how to speak, for I am only a boy" (Jeremiah 1:6). I know I need to do something but that's not what I know how to do. Don't want to learn either!

The unnerving thing about seeking the mind of God is that when we find it, it isn't necessarily what *we* had in mind. God has big plans; we make little plans. God speaks to us, as he spoke to the prophet Elijah, in, ". . . a still small voice" (1 Kings 19:12, RSV), and we sit still and think small. And wonder why our life is like that.

But, God doesn't yell at us. He just keeps whispering in our ear what he has in mind.

In fairness to Jeremiah and to us, our reticence is understandable. The theologian Paul Tillich wrote that "It is safe to say that a man who has never tried to flee God has never experienced the God who is really God."[7] Jeremiah *heard* God. He just didn't believe in God, so he didn't believe in Jeremiah. ". . . I am only a boy. " I can't do that, he said.

What we have here is life from two points of view: God's and ours. God sees who we are, who he made us to be, and all the possibilities in that. We see ourselves for who we are, what we've made of our lives, and all the limitations in that.

Jeremiah was well aware of his limitations. He wasn't making excuses. He was being honest about *himself!* He *couldn't* do what he felt called to do alone. What he was missing, what

46

we too often miss, is that we're *not* alone. The God who calls us is also the God who goes with us.

So God said to Jeremiah: "Do not say, 'I am only a boy' ..." (Jeremiah 1:7). *Don't sell yourself short, Jeremiah!*

That's a term from the stock broker. "Selling short" means that you *don't* believe in the stock you are buying and the company it represents. You sell it at today's price on the assumption that you can buy it at a lower price tomorrow. If the company fails, you succeed! If the company loses money, you make money! If the company cuts its dividend, you reap big dividends. That's sometimes a good way to invest in stocks, but it's never a good way to live. If I sell myself short in life that means that I'm betting against myself. The only way to be right about myself is to be less than I could be.

Psychologists tell us that one of the biggest barriers to getting well is getting used to being sick: used to being less than we could be. It not only seems normal; it feels secure. The primary job of the therapist is to help us realize our mistake.

Kushner says: "There is an old Yiddish saying, 'to a worm in horseradish, the whole world is horseradish.' That is, if we have never known an alternative, then we assume that the way we are living, with all of its frustrations, is the only way to live."[8] God says there's a better way! Maybe you *are* only a boy but I am God! The God who made you. The God who wants to make you what you could be, what you were made to be.

What he made Jeremiah was a prophet.

The question is what does God want to make of you and me?

One thing's for sure. He wants to make you and me people for whom life is worth living forever to the Glory of God, and for the joy of it!

---

1. *The Book of Confessions,* Presbyterian Church (U.S.A.).
2. *Presbyterian Hymnal* 485 (Westminster/John Knox Press, 1990).

3. Quoted by John Powell, S.J. *Fully Human Fully Alive* (Argus Communications, 1976) p. 7.

4. Donald T. Kauffman. *The Treasury of Religious Verse* (Fleming H. Revell, 1962).

5. Harold Kushner. *When All You've Ever Wanted Isn't Enough* (Summit Books, 1986) p. 28.

6. *Ibid.,* p. 29.

7. *The Shaking of the Foundations.* New York: Charles T. Scribner's Sons, 1948, p. 42.

8. Kushner, *op. cit.,* p. 22.

Crackpots

In a recent "Dennis the Menace" comic in the *Lima News*, Dennis' line to his mother is: "Before I tell you what happened, remember I'm just a little kid."

My line to *you* this morning is: "Before I tell you about Jeremiah, remember I'm just a preacher." I'm just a messenger.

Jeremiah, the prophet of God, was just a messenger. Jeremiah said to God, "I don't know what to say." God said, "I'll tell you what to say!" And what God said is what Jeremiah said.

Jeremiah's message to the people of Israel, eventually included in the *Bible*, which is *God's message to you and me,* was this: "You're a bunch of crackpots!" I said I'm only a messenger! Like Jeremiah, I'd just as soon not deliver that message from the Lord but there it is: "Each of you is a crackpot, *and so am I!*"

How so? The first thing to remember is that the word "crackpot" was around a long time before anybody used crack or smoked pot. If you do either then "crackpot" might be as good a term as any to describe your actions, but that's not specifically what I'm getting at. According to *The Random House Dictionary of the English Language* the word "crackpot" is defined as: "a person who is eccentric, unrealistic, or

49

insane." As an adjective "crackpot" means: "eccentric, impractical, insane, crackpot ideas." All of that might apply but it's still not quite what I'm getting at.

It's the derivation of the word that relates to what God says about life through the prophet Jeremiah. The word "crackpot" is an informal or colloquial word which literally means: cracked pot, a pot with a crack in it; with "pot" being an archaic expression for "head." So a "crackpot" is one with a "cracked pot," a crack in the head through which common sense has run out.

It's really not a very nice word. It's usually applied by us to people who are more in need of our sympathy and care and our support than a "label," but it's an apt word for today so long as we apply it to ourselves. Because through Jeremiah God says of the people of Israel they are like "cracked pots." ".... My people have committed two evils (God says): they have forsaken me the fountain of living water, and (they have) dug out cisterns for themselves, *cracked cisterns* that can hold no water" (Jeremiah 2:13).

In a dry and arid part of the world where your backyard is never going to be ankle deep in mud the way it is in an Ohio spring, that's a vivid image. Because in Jeremiah's part of the world, water is clearly life itself; without it you die. Any vessel that is designed to capture water and hold it for use but is cracked is less than useless, and perhaps a danger to the owner who is depending on it to collect the water he needs to live, to hold this water of life. It's a danger because the water drains away through the cracks. So whether you've carved out a large cistern in the stone or just put a pot on the porch to catch the rain — a cracked pot is no-good.

And so, as *The New Oxford Annotated Bible (NRSV)* puts it: "The Lord calls upon the heavenly assembly (all of heaven) to witness the folly unprecedented ... of a people who forsake the *fountain of living water* for the stagnant water at the bottom of leaky cisterns."[1]

"Be appalled, O heavens, at this, be shocked, be utterly desolate, says the Lord ..." (Jeremiah 2:12). This is nuts!

Insane! Without sanity! Without sense! They are acting, they are living, like a bunch of cracked pots and their lives don't hold water. ". . . They have forsaken me, the fountain of living water" (Jeremiah 2:13), the water of life, for whatever's left in a cracked pot. That is, perhaps, the image Jesus had in mind in the story from John when it says he was at Jacob's well with the Samaritan woman. Jesus said to the woman: "Everyone who drinks of the water that I will give them will never be thirsty. The water that I will give will become in them a spring of water gushing up to eternal life" (John 4:13-14).

When the woman asked for some of this living water, this water for living, Jesus didn't just give her a cup and say: "Here, have some." Instead he told the woman about her life. He asked her to look at her life and how she was living it. To look at how the cracks in her life meant her life didn't hold water. That's what Jeremiah was asking the people of Israel to do. To look at their lives (not their pottery). To look at what held water, at what made sense and what didn't.

Last week I prayed over the chicken dinner at a meeting of the Lima Area Labor-Management Citizens Committee. That's an organization in our community devoted to making sure that the relationships between people who make decisions in business, and the people who make things in business, make sense. It's just good business to do that these days!

One of the speakers, talking about our community, said that right now in terms of business opportunities and community development and labor-management relations, "We have the chance of a lifetime!" I want to turn that cliché around: *A lifetime is the only chance we have!* Jeremiah wanted to turn his people around. Much the same way many business people want to turn their way of doing business around.

Another speaker at that meeting was talking about "the total quality movement" in American business. The father of that movement, you could call him the prophet, is W. Edwards Deming. Deming gets right to the point. He says to business people: "Survival is not mandatory." Jeremiah said the same thing to the people of Israel. You don't *have* to live!

51

Deming has talked for years about the "transformation" of American business. But our speaker said that he now feels that isn't strong enough a term. Now he wants to talk about "metanoia" in American business. That's a biblical term! "Metanoia" is a word you can find on the lips of John the Baptist and the lips of Jesus, neither of whom had an M.B.A. It meant REPENT!

This hard-nosed international business consultant is beginning to sound a lot like a hard-nosed messenger of God named Jeremiah! Repent, he says! Not, make a list of everything you're doing wrong; that's bad business. No one's interested in that, not even God. Instead turn around and start doing things right! As a bumper sticker I saw this week put it: "If you're heading in the wrong direction, God allows U-turns!" Repentance — "metanoia" is going another way when the way you're going is going nowhere or worse. It's good for business, and good for life.

At the meeting they gave us a sheet called "Table Talk," things business people need to think about and talk about. It read, in part; "What are your senses (touch, smell, sight, hearing, intuition!) telling you about: the things that are breaking down . . . falling apart . . . going away. The things that are in chaos . . . disorder . . . turbulence . . . fluctuation. The new things that are emerging . . . coming forth . . . becoming evident!" That's more than a good way to look at doing business; that's a good way to look at living life. Asking yourself, what are the broken cisterns in my life? What doesn't hold water anymore? What crackpot things am I doing with the only life I have? A lifetime is the only chance we have. In the business of life have we gone "after things that do not profit?" to quote Jeremiah (Jeremiah 2:8).

How about it? Does life hold water for you? God wants it to. He wants your life *now* to ". . . become a spring of water gushing up to eternal life" (John 4:14). A life worth living — forever. It says so, right there in Jeremiah.

Don't miss it. We tend to read through our reality. We know how bad it can be, so we tend to hear how bad it will be, as though God is simply angry at us. Not so. Faced with the crackpot ways of his people God calls on all of heaven to be ". . . appalled, . . . shocked, . . . (and) utterly desolate." Jeremiah wants us to know that God is totally devastated and distraught that things should be so unlike what they could be in our lives. God isn't out to get us; he wants us to get it, and to live. Not a crackpot existence, with life just dribbling away through the cracks, but a full existence, full of living water which is God himself.

One simple way to get at that, and I'll quit. Ask yourself: *What are the assumptions I live by?* If I get out of bed in the morning it's a good bet that my feet will hit the floor and not the ceiling. That's a good assumption that holds water, at least as long as the law of gravity holds. I can live by that.

But what assumption do I live by in my relationships with other people and with God? What do I expect out of life? What do I expect out of my relationship with God? Is that what I get?

On Friday night I was the one who had to go up to Little Caesar's on Allentown Road and pick up the pizza. Because I had gone up on Cable Road, I had to turn right onto Allentown and then I needed to make a left turn to get into Little Caesar's. There was a lot of Friday night traffic and the cars just kept coming and coming and coming and I kept sitting and sitting and sitting and the pizza was getting colder and colder and colder . . . you've been there? Finally, there was a space between cars and I was going to get through it. But just as I began to make my left turn, in the intersection just ahead of me a car pulled out and around and right in front of me, and I just knew if I didn't make it now all those other cars were going to catch up — and I said — I'm not going to tell you what I said. Let's just say *I made an assumption!* Just as I said what I said, the other car stopped and waved me on! My blood pressure and my life were based in that moment on my assumption.

What are your assumptions about life; and about the people that you have to live it with? I promise you, if you ask that honestly you'll find a few "crackpot" assumptions. It's time to change them — and live!

---

1. *The New Oxford Annotated Bible* NRSV (Oxford University Press, 1991) p. 962 O.T.

The Potter Almighty

"I believe in God the *potter* almighty, maker of heaven and earth." That's the beginning of The Apostles' Creed, as Jeremiah might have written it: I believe in God who has created heaven and earth, and you, and me, *like a potter* at work at a potter's wheel.

That's a biblical image that still makes sense for you and me. At craft shows, in art classes, in hobby shops, you can still find a potter's wheel. And you can take classes in making pottery. If you do, you'll find that these days the potter's wheel has an electric motor, with variable speeds and is run by electricity. In Jeremiah's day the potter's wheel was made of stone and run by foot power. A small stone, on which the pot was made, was connected to a lower, larger stone that the potter turned with his feet. The potter literally had to throw his whole body into throwing a pot. Leaning over the wheel, kicking with his feet, forming the clay with his hands. That's what the potter was doing on the day Jeremiah came to call.

After watching for a while, Jeremiah said that's what God's been doing all along. God, like a potter at his wheel, is at work in his world, shaping, forming, stretching, pushing, pulling us into shape. And not just any shape. Into God's shape. God's form. God's image. (See Genesis 2:7.) In the creation story in Genesis when it says that "...the Lord God *formed* man from the dust of the ground ..." the Hebrew words suggest a potter forming or molding clay.

And the prophet Jeremiah would have known the psalmist's words: "O Lord, our Sovereign, how majestic is your name in all the earth! ... When I look at your heavens, the work of your fingers, the moon and the stars that you have established; what are human beings that you are mindful of them, mortals that you care for them? Yet you have made them a little lower than God, and crowned them with glory and honor" (Psalm 8:1, 3-5).

Lew Smedes puts it this way: "Common clods of clay we are, (yet) God invests his gift to humankind with us."[1]

God's doing his thing with us and for us on the potter's wheel that we call life. As a hymn that I love says: "God is working his purpose out as year succeeds to year ... God is working his purpose out, and the time is drawing near; nearer and nearer draws the time, the time that shall surely be, when the earth shall be filled with the glory of God as the waters cover the sea."[2]

Watching the potter at work at his wheel Jeremiah perceived God at work in his world: even in Jeremiah's world which according to Jeremiah wasn't too different from our world in the way people lived with each other and with God.

Jeremiah perceived two things down at the potter's place.

First, *that God's in charge of this world.* The theological term for that is the "Sovereignty of God": the "rule" of God. Jeremiah says: "... The word of the Lord came to me: can I not do with you, O House of Israel, just as this potter has done? ... just like the clay in the potter's hand, so are you in my hand" says the Lord (Jeremiah 18:5-6).

Jeremiah perceived in the potter's work the primary place of God in the affairs of people. That whatever we're doing, what God is doing is what will be "on earth as in heaven" in good time.

That belief is very Presbyterian. It is, perhaps, one reason that Presbyterians have historically been so willing to risk so much for the life of this world. We believe that this world and our lives are in God's hands. And that he handles us with care.

On the cover of our weekly church *Newsfold* recently, in remembrance of Independence Day, we printed some facts and figures about the men who signed the Declaration of Independence. Men who changed the whole world as they put their lives on the line.

The article notes that "They were not wild-eyed radicals." Thank goodness, because a lot of them were Presbyterians! Of those 56 men who pledged their lives, their fortunes and their sacred honor to the cause of freedom, 12 were Presbyterians.

They did what they did "with a firm reliance on the protection of divine providence;" (says the Declaration), with a sense of certainty that God would see them through; that he was in charge. That ". . . in the course of human events . . ." there is a heavenly potter who, having created all men equal, is still active in creation, working his purpose out. Molding us, making us, into the likeness of God.

One of those men was the only minister to sign on the dotted line, Presbyterian minister, The Reverend John Witherspoon. He and they put their hand to that document, secure in the belief that they were held in the hand of God. That come what may God's purpose for his people would be served and advanced by what they were doing.

Jeremiah's message to the people of Israel was that God's purpose for his people would be served and advanced if they were to *stop* doing what they were doing! That's the second thing that was clear to Jeremiah that day in the potter's shop. *That our will is not always God's will.* During the American Civil War when asked if he thought God was on his side, Abraham Lincoln responded: "I am not so much concerned as to whether God's on my side as to whether I am on his side" (source unknown). Another time he said: "In the present Civil War, it's quite possible that God's purpose is something different from the purpose of either party."[3]

God's purpose is not always the purpose we had in mind. And when we are at cross purposes with the will of God, God's still at the wheel like the potter who when "the vessel he was making of clay was spoiled (in his hand) . . . reworked it into another vessel as seemed good to him" (Jeremiah 18:4).

The word that Jeremiah heard from the Lord and spoke to the people of Israel was that they were about to get a good working over. That the pot on the wheel, the people in their lives, were not acceptable to God, the potter, in the shape they were in. God said to Jeremiah ". . . when you tell this people all these words, and they say to you, 'Why has the Lord pronounced all this great evil against us? What is our iniquity? What is the sin that we have committed against the Lord our God?' Then you shall say to them: it is because your ancestors have forsaken me, says the Lord, and have gone after other gods and have served and worshiped them, and have forsaken me and not kept my law; and because you have behaved worse than your ancestors, for here you are, every one of you, following your stubborn evil will, refusing to listen to me" (Jeremiah 16:10-12).

Throughout his writings Jeremiah lays it on the line with respect to the people's selfishness and greed, oppression of the weak and poor, sexual immorality, abusive business practices, self-indulgence, and self-serving ways even in their serving of God.

You're serving God in none of this, says Jeremiah. The potter is not pleased with the pot on his wheel. "Thus says the Lord, look (pay attention!), I am a potter shaping evil against you and devising a plan against you. Turn now, all of you from your evil way, and amend your ways and your doings" (Jeremiah 18:11).

You can take that two ways: *as a threat* if you perceive that the potter's plan goes against what you had in mind. And that if you keep living the way you've been living you'll eventually be "up against it"; or worse, up against God. Or you can take it *as reassurance* that in this world where there is so much wrong God has every intention of setting it right. As the hymn puts it: "That though the wrong seems oft so strong, God is the ruler yet."[4]

Jeremiah doesn't mean that every evil that befalls us is caused by God to control us. That is simply not so and never said. He does mean that the evil that befalls us because of the evil that we do is *used* by God to correct us. That the wheel is turning, life is taking form, and *we* are called to turn toward life and away from death. "Turn now, all of you from your evil way and amend your ways and your doing" (Jeremiah 18:11).

That's what it means to "repent." Literally, to turn a different way. To be "returned" into the form that the potter intends. And to live life praying as Jesus himself prayed to God as he faced the cross: ". . . not my will but yours be done" (Luke 22:42).

To pray as Jesus taught us to pray: ". . . Thy will be done on earth as it is in heaven" (Matthew 6:10). And then to live life as in the words of the old hymn: "Have thine own way, Lord! Have thine own way! Thou art the potter; I am the clay. Mold me and make me, after thy will, while I am waiting, yielded and still."[5]

So, in the still of this moment, what shall we say?

For some reason the committee that chose the lesson from Jeremiah chose not to tell us what the people said. They left out the last verse in this section. But that which is too often left unsaid in our lives needs to be said, on occasion, so we can hear ourselves say it.

Jeremiah writes: "But they say, 'It is no use! We will follow our own plans, and each of us will act according to the stubbornness of our evil will' " (Jeremiah 18:12).

The potter is at his wheel. The wheel is life. It's turning. What do *you* say?

---

1. Lew Smedes. *How Can It Be Alright When Everything's All Wrong?* (Harper and Row, 1992) p. 71.

2. *The Hymnbook,* 500 (Presbyterian Church in the United States, 1955).

3. Martin Marty. *Righteous Remarks,* (quoting Abraham Lincoln), p. 65.

4. *The Presbyterian Hymnal,* 293 (Westminster/John Knox Press 1990).

5. *The Hymnbook,* 302 (Presbyterian Church in the United Staets, 1955).

Proper 19
Pentecost 17
Ordinary Time 24
Jeremiah 4:11-12, 22-28

Don't
Be Stupid

I ordered a new book this week. Hope it comes soon. Because *God* needs to read it! It's called *Your Executive Image.* As **C**EO of all that is, that's **C**reator, **E**xecutive, **O**verseer; as CEO of anything and everything that matters to you and me, God needs to keep up appearances. And it really doesn't do God's image any good for him to go around calling people "stupid children" (Jeremiah 4:22).

Yet, Jeremiah tells us, God said of his people in Israel ". . . My people are foolish, they do not know me; *they are stupid children,* they have no understanding. They are skilled in doing evil, but do not know how to do good" (Jeremiah 4:22, NRSV)

In his attempt to get our attention, the call of God to you and me is: *Hey stupid!* A childish taunt you'd expect on a school yard; not what you'd expect from God. But there it is. Hey stupid, are you listening to me? says God.

Driving to the hospital last week I was listening to WCIT Radio program's "Cover Story." Anne Nasha was interviewing Victoria Seitz, the author of *Your Executive Image.* Seitz said something that might help us understand what God said. She said that people who speak in public should always remember that the most important thing is not *what* you say but *how* you say it.

Sometimes you have to say things people don't want to hear, just like sometimes a parent has to say things a child doesn't want to hear, like: "It's the first day of school; get up," or "It's time to do your homework," or "It's time for bed," or "It's time to do the dishes," or "It's time to cut that out — that's stupid." When you have to say something someone doesn't want to hear, Seitz says, *how you say it* is just as important and maybe more important than what you say.

Actually, God must've already read the book, because everything God says, he says in love; even "*Hey* stupid!" Hey you; don't be stupid! It'll cost you your life.

Elbert Hubbard once observed that everyone is a darned fool at least five minutes a day; *wisdom* (he said) consists in not exceeding the limit. Jeremiah's message to the people of God was that their five minutes was up. In their foolishness, in their lack of wisdom, in their stupidity, they had exceeded the limits of life and it would cost them their life. *That's stupid!* and it doesn't *have* to be!

If you want to improve your image read Seitz's book. If you want to live in the image of God read God's Book. Don't just listen to the spin doctors, who tell us how to make things *look* good; listen to the soul doctor, by whom all things were made good, who, as the psalmist put it, is the one ". . . Who forgives all your iniquity, who heals all your diseases, who redeems your life from the pit, who crowns you with stead-fast love and mercy, who satisfies you with *good* as long as you live . . ." (Psalm 103:4-5).

The people of Israel didn't listen. Jeremiah writes: "Although they *say* 'as the Lord lives,' yet they swear falsely. O Lord, . . . You have struck them but they felt no anguish; you have consumed them, but they refused to take correction. They have made their faces harder than rock; they have re-fused to turn back" (Jeremiah 5:2-34).

God says go this way and live; we go our own way and die. *Isn't that stupid?* As a matter of fact, *yes!* Said God: ". . . They are stupid children . . . they are skilled in doing evil, but do not know how to do good" (Jeremiah 4:22). How stupid can you be? To live a life that's less than it could be, instead of a life that's more than you ever dreamed it might be.

God's not calling names; he's calling us to life! That's the name of a new book by Rabbi Harold Kushner, *To Life! L'chaim! To life!*

Kushner writes: "The uniqueness of the human being is captured in the phrase that we are 'created in the image of God.' We have a moral dimension. We can be good or bad, where animals can only be obedient or messy.

(He says) "When Charles Darwin shocked the conventions of the 19th century with his theory that human beings were related to animals and did not represent a special creation, someone asked Darwin, 'Is there anything unique about the human being?' Instead of talking about upright posture or brain cavity size, Darwin answered, 'Man is the only animal that blushes.'

(Kushner goes on:) "To recognize that we have done wrong, to recognize that more might have been expected of us than we delivered, is part of the uniqueness of the human being. No other creature can do that. Animals (and little children) can realize that they are about to be punished for something they did, but only mature human beings can judge themselves."[1]

God's call is to maturity, to good judgment in the life he has made; to living it long and living it well; learning how to do good and not evil. God wants you and me to be like the Apostle Paul who wrote to the church in Corinth, which was beset by stupid, childish squabbles: "When I was a child, I spoke like a child, I thought like a child, I reasoned like a child; when I became an adult, I put an end to childish ways" (1 Corinthians 13:11). I grew up. I took responsibility for myself and my life.

Neither Paul nor Jeremiah, by the way, is saying that children are stupid, or that a child being childish is stupid. They are addressing us adults with the message that stupidity comes in holding onto childish ways in adult situations: situations calling for maturity of mind and responsible action.

Both Paul and Jeremiah would have agreed with General Omar Bradley who wrote: "Ours is a world of nuclear giants and ethical infants. We know more about war then we know about peace, more about killing than we know about living. We have grasped the mystery of the atom and rejected the Sermon on the Mount" (Source unknown).

When I was flying to New York a couple of weeks ago I caught up on some reading. I don't remember specifically what I read that prompted it, but I wrote a note to myself on my ticket envelope. It said: as a society we are moving now from the notion that no one is responsible for anything, to the more serious notion that there is nothing to be responsible for. Anything goes — any time, any place.

Dr. Tom Long of Princeton Theological Seminary quotes a character from a short story by Paul Devries: "There was a time when we were afraid of being caught doing something sinful in front of our ministers. Now we are afraid of being caught doing something immature in front of our therapists."[2]

Jeremiah thought there was a great deal to be responsible for in this world, and we're the only ones around to take responsibility.

The essence of good therapy, by the way, is to help us learn to take responsibility for ourselves, and to *not* take inappropriate responsibility for the actions of others. To borrow a phrase from Fagin in the musical *Oliver,* we are called to be those who are "... reviewing the situation," taking a look at our lives, taking responsibility and living responsibly. Anything else is just plain stupid.

And what does a stupid life, a life lived stupidly, look like?

If you're a parent, check out Ann Landers' column in a recent *Lima News,* on "How To Be A Stupid Parent:

- Discipline only when you lose your temper.
- Remain aloof.
- If your children do something wrong, never let them forget it.
- Give your child all the spending money he wants.
- Compare your child with someone else to make him smarten up.

•Always argue in front of the kids as to what they should and should not be allowed to do.

•Make all (their) decisions for them.

•Never trust the little sneaks. If they don't turn out well, it won't be your fault."[3]

Mohandas Gandhi said that these are the things that destroy life — the stupid things:

"politics without principle,
  pleasure without conscience,
  wealth without work,
  knowledge without character,
  business without morality,
  science without humanity,
  worship without sacrifice." (Source unknown)

Gandhi puts it in modern language; God put it in eternal language. The ten commandments could just as well be known as the ten "don't be stupids."

How stupid can we be? Go back and read Ann Landers' list and Gandhi's list and God's list this week.

I went back and read an editorial from *The Wall Street Journal* recently. It was placed as an advertisement for *The Journal* in the *New York Times* (January 8, 1992) with the headline: "When Was The Last Time You Had A Good Conversation About Sin?" The journal notes: "Sin isn't something that many people, including most churches, have spent much time talking about or worrying about through the years of the (sexual/social) revolution. But we will say this for sin: it at least offered a frame of reference for personal behavior. When the frame was dismantled, guilt wasn't the only thing that fell away; we also lost the guidewire of personal responsibility."

We are responsible for our lives. Personally responsible. God gives life, but *we* live life! How are you living? Responsibly in everything? Or stupidly in some things?

It's said that a woman rushed up to the famous violinist Fritz Kreisler after a concert and cried, "I'd give my life to play as beautifully as you do." Kreisler replied, "I did."[4]

65

We all live our life for something. We all *give* our life for something. God loves you. So he tells you: *don't be stupid!*

---

1. Harold Kushner. *To Life!* (Little, Brown, Inc., 1993) pp. 184-5.

2. *Theology Today,* July, 1993, p. 166.

3. Ann Landers, *Lima News,* August 28, 1993.

4. *Bits and Pieces.* (date unknown)

Salve To
Soothe Our Souls

"My joy is gone, grief is upon me,
   my heart is sick . . . I mourn,
   and dismay has taken hold of me.
   Is there no balm in Gilead?" (Jeremiah 8:18, 21-22).

Is there no salve, no soothing ointment, no medicine for our souls?

The hymn we'll sing after the message says there is: "There *is* a balm in Gilead to make the wounded whole. There *is* a balm in Gilead to heal the sin-sick soul."[1]

That's what we have in this passage from the prophet Jeremiah that my Bible describes as a "lament over Judah."[2] What another editor titles: "The Prophet Mourns For The People." A "sin-sick soul." Jeremiah's soul; a soul sick of sin. Sick of everything that separates us from one another, from God and even from ourselves.

Jeremiah so personifies *that* part of the human condition that we named it for him. The word for the words spoken by such a soul as Jeremiah's is "jeremiad." The dictionary defines a jeremiad as: "a lamentation; (or) mournful complaint."[3] That's Jeremiah: a mournful complainer! One who laments even as he lambasts the situation of his people. Who cries as he cries out the wrath of God. One who is sorry for the sorry state of affairs *in* which he is called to minister, but *to* which he must still speak the truth. Jeremiah speaks the truth in tearful lamentation and in tender love.

Recently as the Lima community dealt first with the senseless death of a Lima Senior High student, apparently by murder, and then the senseless death of a second Lima Senior High School student shortly after, I was called and asked to be one of several pastors at the high school on Friday who would just listen and talk to some students. Students whose souls were sick of what was happening to their friends.

I listened. I listened if only because like Jeremiah I found myself called to be in a situation where I said to God and anyone else who would listen, in Jeremiah's words: "... I do not know how to speak" (Jeremiah 1:6). What can I say? So I listened. After all, what would the white pastor of a westside church have to say to mostly black kids of southside Lima about anything — and especially about the deaths of their friends, good kids with good grades and good futures — gone!

Ecclesiastes wrote: "For everything there is a season, and a time for every matter under heaven ..." (Ecclesiastes 3:1).

This was a time to be quiet and listen. For over an hour what I heard, as they talked about their friends and their fears, was also that many of these young people have bought the belief that if they only had what you and I have — money, houses, cars, power — life would be good; they'd have it good. They'd be somebody and then these things wouldn't happen to them. If they only had what you and I have it would be okay. So the big question in many of their lives is "how do I get it?"

Don't be too quick to judge that! After all, the big question for most of *us* is "how do I get *more* of it," and at tax time, "how do I *keep* more of it."

I listened until it was time to speak. I whispered to one of the black ministers who was leading the group, "Do you suppose those kids would want to hear what the white pastor of a 'well-heeled' westside church has to say?" He grinned and said: "Yeah, I think they would." Fortunately he introduced me simply as the pastor of the Market Street Presbyterian Church.

In so many words I told them that I minister to people like you, and not to many people like them. That's the truth. But I also told them that that meant I had something to say to them. Not about them, but about us!

I told them our secret: yours and mine. That sometimes in our pursuit of the American dream, we end up living the American lie. It's a lie we tell ourselves: that who we are depends on what we have, that happiness consists in having more, that our human worth is defined by our net-worth, and that I'll feel better about myself just as soon as I feel better about my checkbook, my career and my car.

It's a lie that we all live, just like them. And what it creates we all live *with*. What it creates is what we're afraid of in this town. What it creates is what they're arguing about in the debate over police protection downtown. We live with the consequences of lying to ourselves about life, and what makes it worth living.

As I listened I wondered is it any wonder that the logic of the street is "Why work for $4.25 an hour in a hot hamburger joint, when I can do a hundred times that selling joints on the street?" That's a hard question to which easy, middle-class answers are no answer at all. Because the essential problem, theirs *and* ours (that verbal separation is part of the problem — it isn't just their problem or "our" problem, it is *our* problem), OUR problem is the problem confronted by Jeremiah. Not *what do we have,* but *what has us?* Biblically put: *what is our god?*

What is the god of our society, the god of our children, the god of our lives? Who is this God who is appeased by the death of children? Jeremiah talks about that. (Read Jeremiah 7:31.) For what or for whom do we live? That's Jeremiah's question. He's crying and he's crying out because the people of Israel have sold their souls to false gods. You can read about them in chapter 6: "For from the least to the greatest of them, every one is greedy for unjust gain; and from prophet to priest, every one deals falsely. They have healed the wound of my people lightly saying, 'Peace, peace,' when there is no peace"

(Jeremiah 6:13-14). Greed is God and the ministers are keeping quiet about it. Everybody's in trouble. Everybody needs to ask, "Who is my God?"

If you want to be philosophical about it you can ask yourself that question as the theological Paul Tillich asked it. Ask yourself, *what is my "ultimate concern"?* Tillich wrote in his *Systematic Theology:* "Our ultimate concern is that which determines our being or not-being . . . (that by which we live or die). Man is ultimately concerned about that which determines his ultimate destiny."[4] When you get right down to it what's your bottom line? Where do you draw the line in your life? What's ultimate? What has you? Are you being had? What is your god?

Maybe that's too philosophical. You'd rather be practical! Then look at another book. It's shorter. And *you* wrote it. It's your checkbook. This is not a plea for the church budget — we'll take care of that when we're ready. Jesus said: ". . . Where your treasure is, there your heart will be also" (Matthew 6:21). If you want to know where your heart is, look at where your treasure is; it follows it. If you want to find your God, look in your checkbook. You've described him in infinite detail. Look not to see what you have but what has you. Not who you are but whose you are.

I told those kids that there is nothing wrong with ambition and hard work and success and even "making it big": the American *dream*. But there is a great deal wrong with making that dream your god, the thing you live for and even die for.

Jeremiah's jeremiad was a plea for a return to the worship of the Lord our God. The nation, Judah, was in disarray. The worship life of the people was directed to other gods, other concerns, and some of what Jeremiah describes would be frankly considered inappropriate reading from this pulpit, even though it's described in detail on headline news.

You'll have to read the details for yourself. Jeremiah describes a nation, a people, a community, set in *their* ways instead of *God's* ways, and the consequences of that way of life. Consequences which a modern Jeremiah would have to say can be found on the front page and in the obituary column of every newspaper, and every night on the evening news.

"Thus says the Lord (in such a world, says Jeremiah) stand at the crossroads, and look and ask for the ancient paths, where the good way lies; and walk in it, and find rest for your souls" (Jeremiah 6:16). What eventually happened to the nation of Israel, to Judah, says Jeremiah, happened because they chose to walk another way.

And so he asks his question:
"Is there no balm in Gilead?"
Is there no salve to soothe our souls?
"Is there no physician there?"
Is there no God whom we can trust with our lives?
There is?

He didn't say that — but that's what he said. "Why then has the health of my poor people not been restored?" (Jeremiah 8:22). What gives?

That is the question Jeremiah cries across the centuries to you and me and the days of our lives.

If you're like me you're like the writer of that hymn sometimes.

"Sometimes I feel discouraged,
    and think my work's in vain,
but then the Holy Spirit revives my soul again."[5]

Black slaves in the South wrote those words after hearing the white Methodist John Wesley preach about Jesus Christ. They believed it. I believe it.

"There *is* a balm in *Lima*
    to make the wounded whole,
there *is* a balm in *Lima*
    to heal the sin sick soul."

Thanks be to God for that balm, who is Jesus, his Christ.

---

1. *The Presbyterian Hymnal*, 394 (Westminster/John Knox Press, 1990).

2. *The New Oxford Annotated Bible* NRSV (Oxford University Press, 1991) p. 976 O.T.

3. *The Random House Dictionary of the English Language* (Random House, 1967) p. 766.

4. Paul Tillich. *Systematic Theology* (The University of Chicago Press, 1951, 1957, 1963, 1967) p. 14.

5. *The Presbyterian Hymnal,* 394.

Lectionary Preaching
After Pentecost

The following index will aid the user of this book in matching the correct Sunday with the appropriate text during Pentecost. All texts in this book are from the series for Lesson One, Revised Common Lectionary. Lutheran and Roman Catholic designations indicate days comparable to Sundays on which Revised Common Lectionary Propers are used.

(Fixed dates do not pertain to Lutheran Lectionary)

Fixed Date Lectionaries *Revised Common and Roman Catholic*	**Lutheran Lectionary** *Lutheran*
The Day of Pentecost	The Day of Pentecost
The Holy Trinity	The Holy Trinity
May 29-June 4 — Proper 4, Ordinary Time 9	Pentecost 2
June 5-11 — Proper 5, Ordinary Time 10	Pentecost 3
June 12-18 — Proper 6, Ordinary Time 11	Pentecost 4
June 19-25 — Proper 7, Ordinary Time 12	Pentecost 5
June 26-July 2 — Proper 8, Ordinary Time 13	Pentecost 6
July 3-9 — Proper 9, Ordinary Time 14	Pentecost 7
July 10-16 — Proper 10, Ordinary Time 15	Pentecost 8
July 17-23 — Proper 11, Ordinary Time 16	Pentecost 9
July 24-30 — Proper 12, Ordinary Time 17	Pentecost 10
July 31-Aug. 6 — Proper 13, Ordinary Time 18	Pentecost 11
Aug. 7-13 — Proper 14, Ordinary Time 19	Pentecost 12
Aug. 14-20 — Proper 15, Ordinary Time 20	Pentecost 13
Aug. 21-27 — Proper 16, Ordinary Time 21	Pentecost 14
Aug. 28-Sept. 3 — Proper 17, Ordinary Time 22	Pentecost 15
Sept. 4-10 — Proper 18, Ordinary Time 23	Pentecost 16
Sept. 11-17 — Proper 19, Ordinary Time 24	Pentecost 17

Sept. 18-24 — Proper 20, Ordinary Time 25	Pentecost 18
Sept. 25-Oct. 1 — Proper 21, Ordinary Time 26	Pentecost 19
Oct. 2-8 — Proper 22, Ordinary Time 27	Pentecost 20
Oct. 9-15 — Proper 23, Ordinary Time 28	Pentecost 21
Oct. 16-22 — Proper 24, Ordinary Time 29	Pentecost 22
Oct. 23-29 — Proper 25, Ordinary Time 30	Pentecost 23
Oct. 30-Nov. 5 — Proper 26, Ordinary Time 31	Pentecost 24
Nov. 6-12 — Proper 27, Ordinary Time 32	Pentecost 25
Nov. 13-19 — Proper 28, Ordinary Time 33	Pentecost 26 Pentecost 27
Nov. 20-26 — Christ the King	Christ the King

Reformation Day (or last Sunday in October) is October 31 (Revised Common, Lutheran)

All Saints' Day (or first Sunday in November) is November 1 (Revised Common, Lutheran, Roman Catholic)

Books In This Cycle C Series

Gospel Set

When It Is Dark Enough
Sermons For Advent, Christmas And Epiphany
Charles H. Bayer

Walking To ... Walking With ... Walking Through
Sermons For Lent And Easter
Glenn E. Ludwig

The Divine Advocacy
Sermons For Pentecost (First Third)
Maurice A. Fetty

Troubled Journey
Sermons For Pentecost (Middle Third)
John Lynch

Extraordinary Faith For Ordinary Time
Sermons For Pentecost (Last Third)
Larry Kalajainen

First Lesson Set

The Days Are Surely Coming
Sermons For Advent, Christmas And Epiphany
Robert A. Hausman

Turning Obstacles Into Opportunities
Sermons For Lent And Easter
Rodney Thomas Smothers

Grapes Of Wrath Or Grace?
Sermons For Pentecost (First Third)
Barbara Brokhoff

Summer Fruit
Sermons For Pentecost (Middle Third)
Richard L. Sheffield

Stepping Inside The Story
Sermons For Pentecost (Last Third)
Thomas G. Rogers